To Dan & Tom —

Remember....

"the grass always looks
greener"

Thanks so much for your
help & friendship...

Kenny Loggins

10-87.

YOUR FRIENDS AND MINE

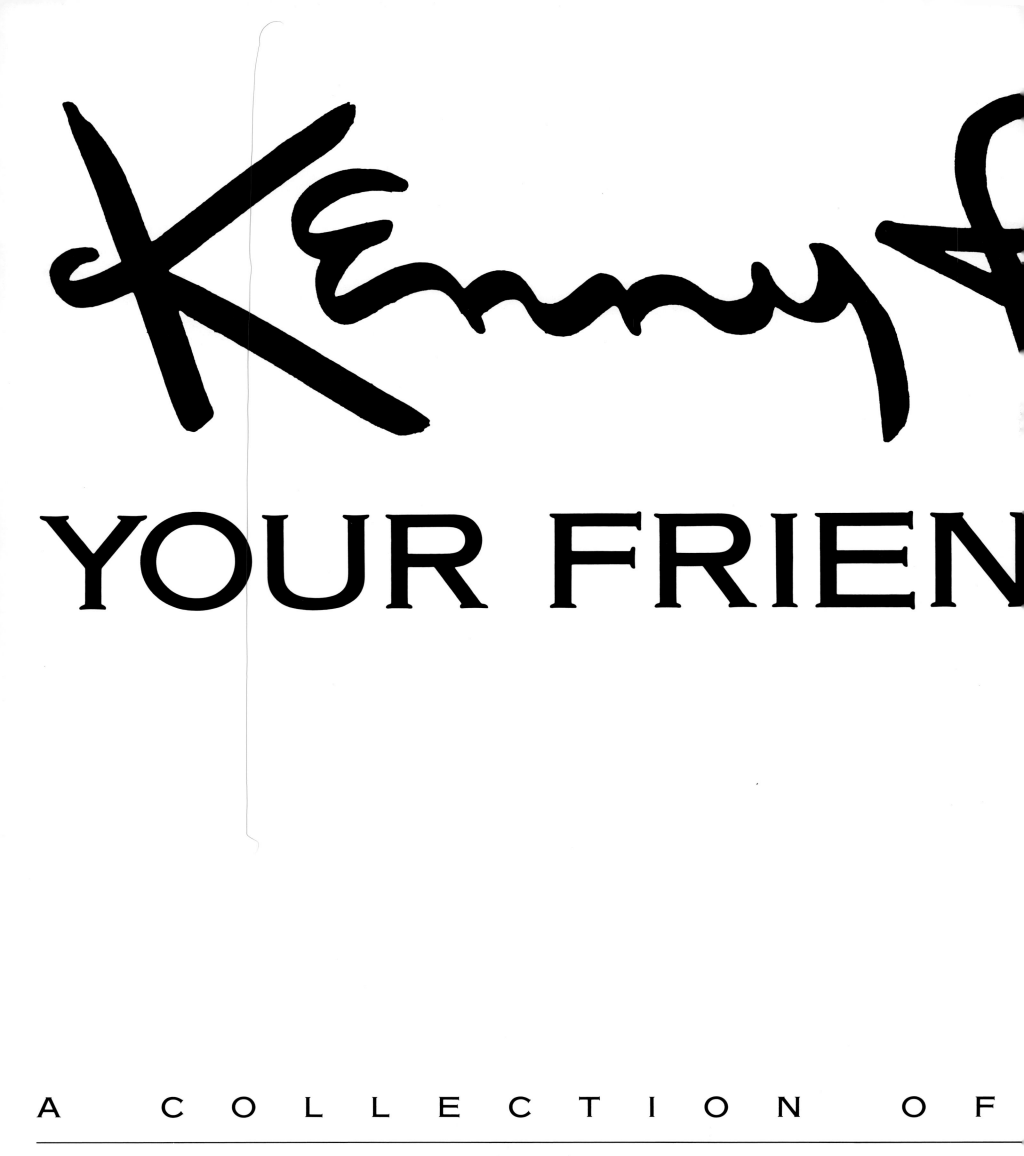

YOUR FRIEN

A C O L L E C T I O N O F

DESIGNED BY JOHN COULTER

Rogers

DS AND MINE

8 0   P H O T O G R A P H S

LITTLE, BROWN AND COMPANY • BOSTON • TORONTO

Books by Kenny Rogers

Kenny Rogers' America
Your Friends and Mine

First Edition

Library of Congress Catalog Card No. 87-16897

Published simultaneously in Canada
by Little, Brown & Company (Canada) Limited

PRINTED IN THE UNITED STATES OF AMERICA

ACKNOWLEDGMENTS

There are many people whose time, effort, and experience helped make this work possible.

BERNARD BOUDREAU

Merely to thank BERNIE BOUDREAU for his assistance in doing this book would be not only unfair but probably unethical as well. It's rare that a person with as much talent as Bernie has will help someone else. He has been my assistant, quality-control coordinator, printer, and technical adviser for the past year. My strength has always been in finding good people who do good work, and in Bernie I certainly found that. I also found a friend. Thanks, Bernie.

Next, thanks to our suppliers, including: BOB SHANEBROOK and EASTMAN KODAK. All black-and-white photographs were made on Kodak Tri-X Pan film, or Kodak T-Max 400 professional film; LOU DESIDERIO, MALIKA DOUGLIN, and the POLAROID CORPORATION for their help and their generous supply of Polaroid types 809 color and 803 black-and-white 8 x 10 instant films; AGFA-GEVAERT, INC., whose Portriga Rapid black-and-white paper and chemicals added a great deal to the richness of the portraits; and TOM CUFFARI and FUJI PHOTO FILM USA, INC., for their beautiful Fuji 100 8 x 10 color film.

And thanks to my friends at LITTLE, BROWN AND COMPANY for having enough faith and confidence in my work to do a second book.

Special thanks then to these individuals whose contributions went above and beyond the call of duty: ROSE LIBRIZZI, makeup artist on the vast majority of the photographs, whose infectious personality, aside from her obvious technical ability, helped set a positive tone for every session. Thanks also to Rose's assistant, JILLIANNE BENNETT; ERWIN SANCHEZ of the Scandal Salon in Westwood, California, for his creative hairstyling on most of the pictures and for being available at the many inconvenient times I needed him; CHRISTIANE ANCTIL of Studio 56, for a magnificent job of retouching many of the photographs; JANICE ABNEY and KAREN VALDEZ, my personal secretaries, for their Bible-salesman approach on the telephone, which made it virtually impossible for many of these celebrities to turn me down; SAM GRAHAM, for taking the words out of my mouth and making them look good on paper; KELLY JUNKERMANN, DAVID OBERG, and ROB PINCUS, for their friendship and additional photographic assistance; KATHY ROBBINS of the Robbins Office, Inc., my agent, for her steadfast belief in the quality of the project when so many times we were told it couldn't be done.

Grateful thanks to the following people for their important contributions, including makeup, hairstyling, or props, to individual photographs: TEDDY ANTOLIN and CHRISTINA SMITH (Liza Minnelli); ARMANDO (Linda Evans); KEVYN AUCOIN (Elizabeth Taylor); LAURIE BAER, DICK KYKER, and JEFF JONES (Morgan Fairchild); KAREN FAYE (Michael Jackson); JOSE EBER (Elizabeth Taylor); JAI (Linda Gray); BOBBE JOY (Dolly Parton, Barbara Mandrell); RAHN McDOW (Barbara Mandrell); ALFONSO NOE (Jaclyn Smith); WYONA PRICE (Dionne Warwick); SHERRI SHORT (Gregory Peck); and JERRY WANKE.

I dedicate this book to my son Christopher, who every day, without knowing it, adds meaning to my life.

YOUR FRIENDS AND MINE

INTRODUCTION

I'M OFTEN AMAZED HOW A MAJOR PROJECT WILL BEGIN NOT WITH A MASTER PLAN OR A GRAND SCHEME, BUT WITH A SIMPLE SUGGESTION. UNTIL A FEW MONTHS AGO, PORTRAIT PHOTOGRAPHY WAS SOMETHING I DID PURELY FOR PLEASURE — MY OWN AND, I HOPE, THE PERSON'S WHOSE PICTURE I WAS TAKING. BUT WHEN A FRIEND CAME TO MY STUDIO IN LOS ANGELES AND SAW SOME OF THESE SHOTS, HE OFFHANDEDLY REMARKED THAT I SHOULD CONSIDER PUBLISHING A BOOK OF PORTRAITS. THE BOOK YOU'RE HOLDING IS THE END RESULT OF THAT CASUAL CONVERSATION, AND I CAN HONESTLY SAY THAT I HAD AS MUCH FUN WITH IT, AND I'M AS PROUD OF THE WAY IT TURNED OUT, AS ANYTHING I'VE EVER DONE.

Your Friends and Mine is a title that works in a number of different ways. To begin with, most of the eighty photos you'll see here are indeed pictures of my friends; if they weren't friends before I photographed them, they are now. Many are such familiar and beloved entertainers and public figures that I imagine people who have never met them or even seen them in person regard them as friends, too. And while some may not have instantly recognizable names and faces, they have the kind of credentials to qualify them as celebrities equal in stature to Michael Jackson, Elizabeth Taylor, or anyone else in this book.

I used no categories or easily defined criteria in deciding who to shoot. I took pictures of pop stars and presidents, actors and athletes, comedians and country singers, pianists and other photographers. In the end, I found that if all of these people have anything in common, it's simply that I respect them, I like them, and I believed they had something special to offer as photographic subjects.

Your Friends and Mine is my second book of photographs; the first, Kenny Rogers' America, was a collection of landscape shots. Although portrait photography is obviously very different, I'm considerably more comfortable with this type of work than I am with landscapes. I've photographed people longer. When I met my wife, Marianne, in the mid-1970s, she was doing a lot of modeling and television commercial work. From helping her and some of her friends with their portfolios, using the small studio and darkroom facilities in our house, I gained experience as a photographer primarily in an indoor, controlled-light situation, along with some outdoor work using long lenses and selective focus. It was then that I got into a habit I've retained ever since: I would take a picture and immediately develop and print it, so I could see the end result within a matter of a few hours. It's always been my style to get things done as quickly and efficiently as possible.

Before meeting Marianne, I'd been an amateur photographer for most of my adult life. I'd used any number of different cameras, from the elementary Brownie Hawkeye through an Argus C-3 and a Hasselblad 2¼ x 2¼. Photography grew from an occasional hobby into a passion. And in the ten years that Marianne and I have been married, she has consistently encouraged me to expand my horizons as a photographer. A couple of years ago, as a Christmas present, she arranged for me to have a two-day, private workshop with John Sexton, who had been an assistant to the great Ansel Adams for a number of years.

With John's expert help, I learned a great deal about photographic techniques, such as using the zone system, understanding the range of light, predicting negatives, and the nuances of print manipulation. John also introduced me to large-format photography, and with his help I began shooting pictures with the large-format 4x5 camera, which I used for *Kenny Rogers' America*. But as useful as all of these lessons were, an inspirational piece of advice John gave me may have been even more important.

The first book, like this one, came about fairly unexpectedly. I had taken thirty or forty landscape shots. The guys in my band and other people I knew were very complimentary, and someone said, "You know, Kenny, you should do a book." And all of a sudden I *was* doing a book.

What was funny about it was the fact that I was having so much fun with my photography—until I signed the book contract. Then I got absolutely depressed. All of a sudden I realized that now people would be looking at my pictures. Before that, I thought my work represented a certain degree of technical knowledge, and knowledge of composition. But once I realized that the pictures would be closely scrutinized by others, they began to look very plain and ordinary to me. I started second-guessing my ability as a photographer, because there's no getting around it: once you have a book published, you *are* a photographer. It was *very* depressing.

I called John Sexton, and his advice was simple. "If you shoot what you like," he said, "you'll like what you shoot. If you photograph things that interest you, you'll have an inherent sense of how to enhance those subjects." John's philosophy played a crucial part in pulling me out of my slump, and I've tried to apply it to every picture I've taken since.

Kenny Rogers' America was a vital step. I had never worked with a large-format camera before, and believe me, it's a totally different device from a 35mm snapshooter. For one thing, you have to be very selective about what you shoot. It takes much more time to set up the equipment, mount the camera on a tripod, focus, and fine-tune every element. You have to develop individual negatives; you have to shoot more than one negative, in case you want to adjust your developing time; and you have to process those negatives very, very carefully. It's not as if you finish shooting a roll of film, send it out to Fotomat, get a proof sheet made, and say, "Oh, I like this picture. Let's have a copy of this one."

Since I wanted to do this book of portraits with an 8 x 10 camera, I think the groundwork I laid with the 4 x 5 was indispensable. When you're working with celebrities, you don't have time to practice: you have to do it, and you have to be right. As it was, I soon found that compared to the 8 x 10, the 4 x 5 seemed utterly spontaneous. Everything about the 8 x 10 is slightly more cumbersome than the 4 x 5. The film surface is four times bigger in area, so the lens has to be twice as long to get the same perspective, and camera vibration is four times as much of a problem. Focus also becomes much more critical. With a 4 x 5, I used a 150mm lens; with the 8 x 10, I moved up to 360mm and 480mm lenses. The camera itself was a Calumet. For black-and-white shots, I used Kodak Tri-X and T-Max film, rated at ASA 160. For color shots, I used Fuji 100 film rated at the same ASA, pushed one stop in development, which allowed me to shoot both color and black and white at the same f-stop and provided the contrast and saturation I preferred for color. In most cases, I first used Polaroid film to test lighting, poses, depth of field, and focus, all factors that are critical when using the 8 x 10.

Although this book has always been titled *Your Friends and Mine*, the concept has gone through several stages. When I began work on it, I planned to shoot only couples—not just people who are romantically involved, or members of a family, but people who are related to each other either personally or professionally. Later on I decided to expand the couples concept to include people and their pets. And still later, the idea was to shoot each person in a way that would be unique to him or her, such as Larry Bird with a basketball, Tony Curtis with his paintings, and Liza Minnelli against a New York City backdrop.

It soon became obvious that limiting myself to a single concept would never work, so I used all three. I also realized that I could shoot my subjects in one of three ways: as they see themselves, as the public sees them, and as they've never been seen before. But even with these expanded guidelines, I soon found that it was very, very hard to take over seventy interesting photographs. The first fifteen or twenty were easy; they were creative, they were quick, they were enjoyable. The second fifteen or twenty were more difficult and challenging, and very draining. And the last were, quite frankly, hard work. That had nothing to do with the subjects themselves. It had to do with the ability to continue to be creative and technically adventurous within the boundaries I had prescribed for myself. For example, I used fourteen lights for Rachel McLish, one of the last shots I took; for Whoopi Goldberg, who came much earlier, I used one.

I guess I'd equate it to a woman having a

baby: for the first three months it's new and enjoyable, for the second three months there's a little more discomfort, and at the end, it's sheer pain. And yet, the result makes it all worth it. What's more, that last difficult period is an essential growth process, if you'll excuse the pun; you need it to push you to another level you might never have reached if you'd only done what came naturally and easily to you. I know that was the case for me with *Your Friends and Mine*.

The first person I shot for the book was Michael Jackson. In 1986, I hosted the Grammy Awards telecast in Los Angeles. That night, my son Christopher met Michael backstage. Christopher had always loved Michael. He would even dress like him at home—probably because he doesn't have silver hair and a beard, so he couldn't look like me. As it happened, Marianne sent me some flowers with a little plastic Grammy attached. Unbeknownst to me or anyone else, Christopher took the plastic Grammy, walked into Michael Jackson's press conference, and handed it to him.

The next day, Michael called to tell Christopher how much he appreciated it. He also invited him out to his house to see his animals, so Marianne and Christopher went out to Encino. Michael knew I was a photographer, and he mentioned that he'd like it if I took a picture of him and Christopher together. I called Michael the next day to set up an appointment, and he agreed to come down to the studio.

I told Michael during our first session that I was thinking about doing a book of portraits and calling it *Your Friends and Mine*. I had heard about his chimpanzee, Bubbles, and we did a shot with the chimp and Christopher, and one with Michael and the chimp. Later on Michael and I did another session alone, at his request. That was the start. Michael Jackson's agreeing to be part of the book was, in fact, the jumping-off point for the whole project.

After Michael, I began calling people I already knew well, like Linda Evans and Linda Gray. But it soon became obvious that I'd have to start contacting people I didn't know at all, because the simple fact is that I wasn't close friends with over seventy people who have the stature that I wanted for the book. Once I began getting in touch with other people, I found they were all enthusiastic about it, except for one thing: like me, they hate doing photo sessions; they didn't want to spend all day in a studio, doing three or four setups, changing their clothes several times, constantly having to check their makeup and hair. Those sessions can be pretty tedious.

I started thinking about what I could do to

economize on the time involved, and I realized that as a rule I was only getting one good shot per setup anyway. And since I was only going to use one shot for the book, why put these people through the grueling pace of a normal photo session? That wouldn't be much fun for me or for them. If I could organize properly, they could be in and out in thirty minutes. So I decided to use just one setup, or perhaps two if they had the time. Once we knew what we were going to do, I would take only six black-and-white shots and two or three in color, because once you get beyond that, you trade personal spontaneity for technical quality. Under those conditions, it was amazing how many people were excited about participating.

Whenever I tried to get someone to photograph for the book who I hadn't met before, or someone I'd met but didn't know very well, I made a point of making the initial overture through an intermediary—a mutual friend or business associate. That made it easier for the celebrities to say no, and to be honest, it made it easier for me to be turned down. Some people were reluctant at first. For instance, I'd never met Elton John, but I really wanted to shoot him because he's a flamboyant, magnetic personality and I thought he would add a nice element to the book. I tried a couple of indirect approaches and was turned down. Then one night Marianne and I had dinner with Alana Stewart, who knows Elton. She told us he was invited to a party at her house the next night, and I said, "Great. Would you mind mentioning the book to him?" She did, but apparently Elton just hates having his picture taken. I figured that was the end of it, and I accepted it.

Marianne and I were invited to another of Alana's parties, and when we arrived I met Elton; he immediately apologized for not wanting to be in the book. But as the night went on and we got to know each other, I told him about a dream I'd had where I went to see one of his concerts. He sang a song in the dream called "My Father's Change." It was about my childhood and my relationship with my father, and although it doesn't really exist, it was one of the most beautiful songs I'd ever heard. I think that gave us a remarkable basis for communication, and at the party Elton started playing around at the piano, trying to write the song I'd described. In the end Elton did agree to be in the book, and we developed a relationship I value tremendously.

What made this project so rewarding for me, then, is more than merely the gratification that comes with creating a good photograph. I've also had the chance to make friends with people I might otherwise never have gotten to know. I think it helped that each person could see me not just as a photographer, but as a peer. First of all, there's the curiosity factor. Obviously, I'm much better known for my music than I am for my photography. I think many people accepted the challenge of appearing in the book because of the unique circumstances. It wasn't as if they were working with Scavullo, who's a known commodity, a professional with a certain reputation and particular standards. With me, I think the attitude was, "Well, this will be interesting. I'd like to see what he can do." I had an unusual access to these people, which in turn helped make the book special.

Also, some celebrities are justifiably a little camera shy, and they knew I wasn't some paparazzo lurking in the bushes outside a fancy restaurant, waiting to get a picture of a star at any cost. They knew I'd be protective of their image; I felt a certain responsibility to get a good shot, and if I took a picture that didn't work, I wouldn't use it. Also, I had very few conditions laid out beforehand. I asked people not to wear white: the way I light my photographs, white clothing can result in a loss of richness or detail in the final print. I asked them to bring a choice of clothing if possible, something with texture and that makes some kind of statement about them. I had a wardrobe woman to help me out, as well as a makeup artist and a hairstylist, and if the subject was a woman, I could offer a variety of accessories, such as earrings or bracelets. Other than that, it was anything goes.

As I said earlier, it became apparent to me in the course of the project that there are three ways to photograph people: the way they see themselves, the way others see them, and the way they've never been seen before. I did my best to determine how I wanted to shoot someone before he or she ever came to the studio, but sometimes I felt I owed it to the subject to give him or her that choice as well. Flexibility is essential.

In some cases I deliberately wanted to portray a person in the third of those three ways—something unusual that would reveal a side the public might see only rarely, if ever. When I arranged to shoot Linda Evans, I asked her to dress very casually, because she's usually seen as so glamorous. She came in wearing jeans and a cowboy hat, and at one point I asked her to just throw her leg over the back of the sofa we were using. When she did, she reached down to straighten her tennis shoe, and I took the picture. The result was an exceptional shot. In fact, my assistant, Bernie Boudreau, who's an excellent photographer in his own right and has shot Linda many times before, told me that no one had ever shot her like that before. Again, I think people trust me, and I wouldn't have used that picture if it hadn't turned out well.

I tried in general to let each person dictate the mood of the shot. I rented a big Wurlitzer jukebox for Dick Clark, because it seemed so utterly appropriate for him. Dick Clark is all about music, and how better to personify that than with a neon-lit jukebox full of single records? Even so, I wasn't sure how I'd use it until he got into the studio. As a rule, I won't discuss an idea in advance in any real detail, to preserve a sense of spontaneity at the session itself.

In some cases, my original instinct was the opposite of what the subject wanted to do. I had a shot dreamed up for Priscilla Presley that would be very glamorous and high fashion. But when she got to the studio, she said that while she'd be very happy to do it my way, she'd prefer to do something more plain. It was a perfect example of the different way viewers see a person and the way the individual sees herself. The result, with Priscilla in her simple straw hat, is totally different from the way I saw Priscilla Presley, but it is a beautiful shot. I wanted to offer my subjects enough latitude so they would be proud of the picture, too. If that meant reordering my preconception of someone, so be it.

Whatever the situation, I tried to relax each subject to the point where he or she wasn't posing, per se, although some of the pictures were designed as posed portraits. The great photographer Yousuf Karsh and I had become friends in the course of my last book, and from him I learned a trick he calls "the stolen moment." It involves talking to your subjects to help them gradually lower the barrier that results in a stilted pose; as they talk, their body language becomes more relaxed, and it's possible to catch them at a personal, revealing moment. When I shot Yousuf himself, he wasn't ready to be photographed—he was talking to Rose, the makeup artist—but that's what makes it an unusual picture.

If there's a single focus that my shots have, it's that I love eyes. I love seeing a person's expression with the eyes straight into the camera. There's a wonderful picture by Yousuf Karsh of Pablo Casals. He's playing the cello, and you know it's Casals, but his back is to the camera. Now, I could never have taken that photograph. But Yousuf doesn't just record the image of a person—he shoots the *soul* of a person. By the same token, I'm not comfortable with the kind of experimentation used by a photographer like Annie Leibovitz. She has done some rather bizarre things with some very famous people, but I don't have the nerve, probably because I don't think I'd want to be in that position myself. I saw a shot by her of Whoopi Goldberg sitting in a white enamel bathtub filled with milk, with only her face, arms, and legs visible. It's a great photograph, but never in my wildest dreams could I have taken it. My book is different, anyway; it's more a record of the time I spent in the studio with some friends.

I did try to take a few technical chances. For Ray Charles, I wanted to use a one-second exposure that would show Ray smiling, with his arms crossed, swaying back and forth the way he does. The picture would have movement, but I'd fire the strobe light when Ray was in the middle so his image would be stationary there. We did take that shot, along with four other, more conventional poses that are beautiful, classic Ray Charles. With Little Richard, I used a combination of strobe and tungsten lighting. I lit Richard with a strobe overall and then put a spot tungsten on his right hand, in order to get the movement of his piano playing. This was a decision made on the spur of the moment during the session, and I think it turned out well.

For most of the shots, I used Broncolor Pulso 4 power packs and lights, a system that automatically varies the intensity of the modeling lights with the power of the strobe, thus showing me in advance what the lighting will be in the final shot. In portrait photography, the quality of light from the keylight is crucial; I used a Plume Wafer lightbank for the keylight. By using all three sizes of lightbanks, varying their distance from the subject, and changing (sometimes eliminating) the diffusion panels, I managed to gain quite a bit of control over the feel of the light, from a hot, specular light to a soft wash wrapping around the subject. I also employed a system I call "layered lighting." It's a term that I coined, but it seems so obvious that I can hardly believe no one else has ever called it that. Layered lighting involves using a minimum of four zones, or areas of light: the hard, white rim light; the softer front, or flat light; the back light; and plain black, which is also considered a zone. Put simply, the system allows me to use the various textures and values of light to highlight different qualities of a person's face. The photos of Cesar Romero, Clint Eastwood, and Rachel McLish are good examples of the layered lighting effect.

The vast majority of the pictures were taken in my studio. I prefer to work there, where I can best control the lighting and every other factor. But for various reasons (I can't imagine why, but President Reagan couldn't fit a trip to the studio into his schedule), I occasionally went elsewhere, for instance to Hugh Hefner's home or to Santa Anita racetrack for jockeys Bill Shoemaker and Laffit Pincay, Jr. At first, not having done much location shooting, I worried about leaving some vital piece of equipment behind. I learned to make a checklist of everything I could conceivably need, even including obvious items like film. I numbered and sequenced the list, beginning with the camera and moving down through the synch cord, the cable release, the tripod. I had the list laminated, and if I could have had it surgically attached to my body, I probably would have done that, too. Once the list was done, I never forgot anything.

After the image you want is on film, there's a great deal you can do with it during the printing process. Ansel Adams once said that the negative is the musical score, but the printing is the performance. He used to spend literally days printing a single shot. To use his own analogy, Adams was a true maestro in the darkroom.

Bernie would typically be out the door of the

studio on the way to the darkroom at my house immediately after a session with a celebrity. First we'd process one sheet from each setup, to get an idea of whether we'd want to make adjustments in the development time in order to compress or expand the range of tones or change the highlight detail. If I had a feeling during the session that one shot would be particularly good, we'd mark it and develop it last, so we could use the other negatives to work out whatever bugs there might be in the development process.

As for printing, Bernie, Brad Cole, and occasionally I often spent five or six hours to get a good print of a shot that might have been taken in fifteen minutes. You can use the process called dodging to make an area of the print lighter, or the one called burning to make it darker. You can retouch a print to remove an element you don't like. You can even change the color entirely in sections of the photograph. To get the effect I wanted for the shot of Paul Simon, we later painted in our own color gels on several of the spotlights behind him that had been white, thus altering the transparency.

A few years ago, before I met John Sexton, I never would have been so consumed by the technical details of photography. But as my involvement has increased, so has my thirst for more knowledge and expertise. As I said, photography has grown from an avocation into a serious creative outlet, almost another career. Like music, it gives me a great deal of personal satisfaction. In fact, I get at least as much satisfaction from my photography as I do from my music. What's more, having photography as an outlet takes some of the pressure off my musical career. There are people in the entertainment business, or any business, whose work is 95 percent of their lives. That's all well and good, provided you have a thriving, successful career. But according to that philosophy, when your career is gone, 95 percent of your life goes with it. You have nothing to fall back on.

I prefer to live my life according to the *probability*, as opposed to the *possibility*. The possibility is that I'll be an exception in music; like Frank Sinatra, I'll still be singing in my seventies, and people will still want to hear me. The probability, based simply on the law of averages, is that I won't. Like most everybody else, I could end up as yesterday's news. Quite honestly, my success in music has already lasted longer than I thought it would, longer than I predicted it would—and I'm sure some would say longer than it should have! But if my musical career comes to an end for some reason, I can continue to express myself creatively as a photographer. Photography shows that I'm not one-dimensional, and it's a means by which I can both enjoy today and prepare for tomorrow. Most important, it's something I truly love. And if a fraction of the pleasure I had doing *Your Friends and Mine* is apparent in these pictures, I'll feel I have accomplished something. They may be pictures of other people, but there's a lot of Kenny Rogers in *Your Friends and Mine*, too.

MICHAEL JACKSON

Michael Jackson is unique, both as an individual and as a performer. Yet while I'd been around him many times, I never honestly felt I knew him until we spent a day together in the photography studio.

As I explained earlier, Michael had invited Christopher, my youngest son, to his home to see his zoo. They had such a good time that Michael, who'd heard I was a photographer, suggested I take a picture of him and Christopher in my studio. I told him of my idea for this book and asked him to bring his chimpanzee, Bubbles.

There were maybe twenty-five people in the studio that day, and the chimp was the center of attention. That meant that the focus was off Michael, and I think the relative anonymity gave him a chance to relax. And Bubbles was so human it was almost frightening. He would take Christopher by the hand, walk over to the refrigerator, open it, take out a banana, and hand it to him. Christopher was amazed— we all were.

The session was the first time I'd had a chance to be one-on-one with Michael. It means a lot to me to be able to say that not only do I love his music, but I also like him very much as a person and consider him a friend.

LINDA GRAY

I've known Linda Gray for fifteen years, and I've watched her success as an actress throughout that time. She was one of the first people I called to be in the book.

I was determined to do something original with Linda, as opposed to the standard shot of "Linda Gray of *Dallas*." It helped that she gave me an entire day to experiment with different setups. The result is one of my favorite photographs, one that's deliberately dark and somewhat moody. I printed it lighter once, but there was almost too much information; I just didn't feel it had the same impact as the darker version. But then, it's so subjective: you can give the same negative to five different photographers, and you'll get five different prints. Ansel Adams was right when he said that the negative is like a musical score, but the print is the performance. This is one performance I'm very proud of.

BURT BACHARACH AND CAROLE BAYER SAGER

You know what they say about the best-laid plans of mice and men....

As a rule, I asked people not to wear white for their photo session. In this case, I specifically talked to Carole and said, "Wear whatever you want, but please, no white: it blows out on the camera," meaning that white clothing on a white background can result in a loss of detail in the final print. She said fine—but what she didn't say was that she and Burt wear white in nearly every photograph they're in! For them, white is almost a uniform. So when they showed up in these clothes, that was the end of the discussion—I set up and took the shot. To make the clothes an integral part of the design element, I put a dark wall behind Burt and Carole to make the white stand out.

Despite my reservations about white, I must say that I like the way the picture turned out. There's a cleanness about it, a wholesomeness, which I think reflects Burt and Carole *and* their music. Here's a case where there's a strong relationship between what people do and what they wear.

KIRK DOUGLAS

"They don't make 'em like they used to." You only have to meet Kirk Douglas once to appreciate fully the truth in that statement. That also happens to be the title of a song I recorded for the film *Tough Guys,* in which Kirk and Burt Lancaster play two old hoods getting out of prison after thirty years. I think there's a little of that hood in the *real* Kirk Douglas, too, and there's something in his eyes and just the way he carries himself that separates him from all the other tough guys who sustained careers through the great era of movie-making: *"I'm* Spartacus!"

One thing I'd love to do is photograph Kirk and all of his actor sons together. I'd need a wide-angle lens to do it—there are five of them altogether, and they all have that inimitable, steely-eyed Douglas look. Kirk's got the best dimple, though.

JIMMY STEWART

I literally pushed my friendship with Jimmy Stewart to the limit for four months, with phone calls at least once a week, until I finally got my photo of one of the truly great heroes of our time.

After offering to go to his house or shoot him in my studio, I finally realized that both Jimmy and I would be at the People's Choice Awards in February. So there I stood backstage with my 8 x 10 camera, amidst all the people from *Newsweek*, all the photographers from *Time* and *Life*, waiting my turn. I had no props to work with, just a chair from the commissary with my focusing cloth tossed over it. But Jimmy is an amazing man, surrounded by the aura of what Hollywood is, was, or could ever hope to be.

Probably five hundred pictures were taken of Jimmy Stewart that night. I took four.

PRESIDENT GERALD FORD

The main problem with photographing other people whose schedules are as busy as mine is simply arranging to be in the same place at the same time. In this instance, the first convenient opportunity came under unusual circumstances: President and Mrs. Ford and I were at the home of a mutual friend in Palm Springs, California, attending a fundraiser for the preservation of bighorn sheep. I'd known him casually, and this occasion gave me a chance not only to take his picture but to renew a friendship with someone I admire very much.

I've always seen President Ford as the captain of the football team (of course, he did play at the University of Michigan). Since he's less formal than some other chief executives have been, my idea was to capture him in a less formal setting. I wanted this picture to look as if it were taken in the Fords' own living room.

It didn't take long for the conversation to turn to golf. President Ford's exploits on the golf course are the stuff of legend, and lately I've spent quite a bit of time out there myself, futilely trying to correct my hook swing. We talked about playing together but quickly agreed that the two of us on the same course would constitute a national hazard. Our caddies would have to wear hard hats.

JOHN HUSTON

Something about people who make films intimidates me. Especially people of the stature of John Huston, who has directed several movies—like *The Maltese Falcon, The Treasure of the Sierra Madre,* and *The African Queen*—that are among the best ever made. And then when I remember that he's also a great actor...Well, the good news is that there are only a few people of John Huston's stature.

I found this old Mitchell camera at a rental house in Hollywood (that's another good thing about this town: you can rent anything, anytime). I've seen John on television many times, but lately he's been in a wheelchair, and I didn't realize how tall he was until he stood up: he's six foot two.

Before he arrived, I was concerned that the big camera might overpower him in the shot. But I learned that you have to allow for presence as well as size. This camera could have been twice as big, and John Huston would still have dominated the photograph.

JACLYN SMITH

Jaclyn Smith was stunned when I suggested that her picture be taken with a Harley-Davidson motorcycle and a black leather jacket. Well, I'm not sure *stunned* is the right word. But I assure you it wasn't what she had anticipated. In fact, she was coming from another photo session, where she had been dressed very elegantly.

Jaclyn made me promise to shoot a backup photo, in case this one didn't work. But the more she thought about wearing the leather, the more excited she got about it. The entire time we were doing the alternative setup, she kept saying, "Make sure we have enough time for the motorcycle."

Ah...the secrets we all hide. Jaclyn Smith loves black leather.

DICK CLARK

When I was nineteen years old, I went to Philadelphia to appear on *American Bandstand*. I swear to you, Dick Clark looks exactly the same now as he did then. And he is one of the few people who has managed to remain completely contemporary in music, too, for more than thirty years.

This picture was a tricky photograph to take. I tried first to get an *American Bandstand* logo behind him. The jukebox was certainly appropriate, but we couldn't light it or the colors would have severely washed out. As it was, it required a fifteen-second exposure with no modeling lights and isolation of the keylight on Dick.

By the way, Dick doesn't remember me on the show. I must have been great.

ELTON JOHN

I know this sounds crazy, but this picture began with a dream. I dreamed about an Elton John concert where he sang a song—from start to finish, with lyrics and melody—called "My Father's Change." Elton certainly doesn't know any song by that title, but in the dream it was very vivid and detailed. I saw myself as a little boy, lying in bed as my father got home from work. As he undressed, I could hear the change in his pocket, and that familiar sound assured me that all was right with the world. I must have carried this image in my unconscious for decades.

I met Elton at a party after my attempts to get him for the book through agents and managers had failed. Once I'd personally told him about the dream, I ask you, how could he turn me down? I had no idea what to expect from him when he came to the door, but I loved the cane. And if you look closely, you'll see the ponytail with the bow, the hat, and, of course, the Elton John sunglasses.

JULIE HARRIS

This shot of Julie Harris, who I've loved on television and especially in *The Belle of Amherst* and the earlier *A Member of the Wedding* on Broadway, came from the period of the book when I happened to be shooting a lot of people with their pets. Ever since Linda Gray came in with her very large German shepherd, I was always relieved when a person's pet was small, like Julie's. It required much less paper on the studio floor.

The picture is a good example of Yousuf Karsh's theory of the "stolen moment" approach to photography, which involves talking to the subject and relaxing him or her to the point where you get a shot that looks almost informal, instead of stilted or contrived. There were several other shots of Julie, but to me they all looked posed. I liked this one because she's in midconversation, holding her glasses very casually. And although it was obviously taken in a studio, Julie's gestures make it look as if we were relaxing in her living room.

PRESIDENT RONALD REAGAN

Twenty-six security men, two body checks, and a metal detector proved to me that country singers don't get special treatment when it comes to the President of the United States.

I had made several attempts through friends at the White House to photograph President Reagan. Progress was slow. Ultimately I was put in touch with Larry Speakes, the then White House spokesman, who worked very hard to help me arrange this shoot. Finally, last December, I got a call saying the President would be at the Century Plaza Hotel in Los Angeles if I was still interested. After all the security checks were made, I was led to a room where the picture would be taken.

I determined that I'd use the large windows behind the President as a background, until I was told that if he had his back to the window, the Secret Service would have to shift their snipers to protect him. I had visions of a *Blue Thunder* helicopter coming out of nowhere, something happening, and my being in prison for the rest of my life. It changed my shot —no pun intended!

So there I stood, in the middle of the room, and President Reagan tapped me on the shoulder. I'm not sure what I said, but I *am* sure it didn't make much sense. It was something like, "Oh... Mr. President....How nice to meet you. I've heard so much about you." I can't imagine him not being impressed.

DUDLEY MOORE

Thank God it was Dudley. Newsman Charles Kuralt was doing a segment on my first book, *Kenny Rogers' America,* for his "Sunday Morning" television show, and he wanted to send a crew out to my studio to film me during a photo session for this book. I was a little apprehensive. The last thing I want when I'm taking someone's picture is a lot of people standing around watching and (at least in my mind) second-guessing what I'm doing. It's hard enough trying to break through that comfort barrier alone. But Dudley was great. We had performed together the night before on "The Tonight Show" (we played "Satin Doll"; Dudley's a fine pianist, and I played bass for the first time in years) and had met several other times, so we were totally at ease with each other.

What helped me most was that Dudley is truly crazy—he'll do almost anything. I had two props in mind for the photo: a pair of Roman columns, which I thought he might stand between, and this huge, hand-carved wooden goose. Dudley took one look at the columns and said, "I'd feel a little too important with those. With a goose, I feel I'm on the same level."

I must admit the goose was perfect for Dudley. In fact, I'm sure he struck up a profound personal relationship with it. The smile says a lot.

MORGAN FAIRCHILD

I've known Morgan Fairchild for many years. In fact, I first photographed her in Dallas, Texas, out at Turtle Creek, when she was eighteen. Since this was the first opportunity I'd had to photograph her since those days, I was determined to do something unique.

For some reason, I woke up in the middle of the night thinking about Morgan in a glass bathtub (believe me, my fantasies aren't usually so vivid). Luckily, I found that tub. Then I had someone come in and blow up all these balloons, and I put a mirror and a large bubble machine behind her. The result, I think, was as special as I could have hoped.

When I sent her a copy of the photo, I wrote, "Dear Morgan: I had the touch-up artist put some clothes on you so your mother wouldn't be embarrassed."

ALEXANDER GODUNOV

Some pictures simply demand to be in color. It's not that they wouldn't hold up in black and white; they're just infinitely stronger in color. When I saw Alexander Godunov's great shock of blond hair and that powerful face, I knew color was the only way to go.

I'd have loved to photograph Alexander as a dancer, but I got the distinct feeling that he did not want to be seen that way, which is certainly understandable. Alexander's success as an actor, especially in *Witness* and *The Money Pit*, has made him reluctant to be restricted to the dancer image. I've found myself that you don't always want to be saddled with a particular image. People still want to shoot me with a guitar, and I don't even play guitar anymore.

CATHERINE OXENBERG

I was aware of Catherine Oxenberg before she joined the *Dynasty* cast and became a star. I'd seen a Francesco Scavullo portrait of her and her mother, Princess Elizabeth of Yugoslavia, and was struck by how beautiful they both were. But I'd never met Catherine in person before I called her and invited her to be in the book.

We did two completely different setups, and the results were equally good, I thought, which meant that choosing the shot I'd eventually use was pretty much an arbitrary decision. The way I see it, you can hardly go wrong when you have a subject like Catherine.

We didn't plan to shoot her in her bare feet. But she came to the studio wearing an old pair of Reeboks, and rather than switch to the fancy pair of shoes under the chair, she was more comfortable wearing none at all. What surprised me about Catherine was how soft-spoken and genuinely shy she is. I can remember seeing her interviewed by Joan Rivers recently. When Joan asked her what she'd change about her body, Catherine answered, "Oh, everything." Well, from what I could see, it'd be hard to improve on any part of her. When she signed a copy of this picture for me, she even thanked me for making her look so good. Catherine, it wasn't hard.

BRUCE BOXLEITNER

If you don't recognize this guy, look again. Aside from being my friend, Bruce Boxleitner has also been my sidekick in the "Gambler" movies I've done for CBS-TV. And I can tell you, the man is a cowboy through and through. He came traipsing into my studio with all of his own gear, including the saddle. So this picture is a perfect example of a person photographed exactly as he sees himself, and it's not necessarily the image the public has come to know through his *Scarecrow and Mrs. King* series.

As I look back at some of the pictures in this book, I see a few that I might like to shoot again, given the opportunity to try a different approach. This is definitely not one of them. What you see here is the real Bruce Boxleitner. This picture shows you where his heart is.

BOB HOPE

When I first started these portraits, I wanted to do them all in my studio. This wasn't an egotistical decision; at this point in my career I felt the quality would suffer when I went on location. I quickly learned, however, that to get the people you want—like Bob Hope—you must sometimes adjust, so adjust I did.

My first phone conversation with Bob was alarming. I had met him many times and considered him a friend. Yet when I called, it was as if he'd never heard of me. After five or ten minutes of squirming in embarrassment, I finally figured out that perhaps he thought there was *another* Kenny Rogers who was using the similarity in our names to attract celebrities for a book. I was very relieved when he said, "Oh, Kenny Rogers, the singer!"

This picture was taken on Bob's eighty-third birthday at his home. Just as I was about to shoot it, he asked, in typical Bob Hope fashion, "Tell me, Kenny, how much money can you make going door-to-door with this camera?"

SYLVESTER STALLONE

It's never hard to take a picture of a handsome man! I've known Sylvester Stallone since around the time of the first *Rocky,* which won him an Academy Award. I introduced him to a heavyweight fighter named Lee Canalito, who actually called himself "the Italian Stallion," which of course is Rocky's nickname in the films. Sylvester eventually hired Canalito for another of his movies, *Paradise Alley.*

We've run into each other several times since those days. I'd say we were friendly, but not friends, so I was grateful that Sylvester said yes right away when I called him about the book, and he seemed anxious to be involved. There was just one problem: Sylvester Stallone fills out a suit better than any man I've ever seen. The whole time I was shooting him, I was so conscious of the incredible condition of his body that I found myself holding my stomach in. This was one session I wanted to be over in a hurry.

RAY CHARLES

I think if you were to ask the people who sang on "We Are the World" to name the one singer they were most in awe of, the one they were most proud to be performing with, 99 percent would say Ray Charles. I know I would. My relationship with Ray Charles goes considerably beyond enjoyment of his music or appreciation of his talent. He is actually personally responsible for my being in the music business.

As a sixteen-year-old in Houston, I attended my very first concert and saw Ray Charles, Sam Cooke, and the Drifters. It was quite a bill, and I remember thinking, "What a great thing: you can get paid to make music!" I decided then and there what I wanted to do with my life. Had there been no Ray Charles, I might still be running an elevator in a Houston hotel.

Ray has the warmest smile I've ever seen, and yet he feels uncomfortable posing. I ended up telling him dirty jokes and shooting on the punch lines. Out of five shots, I got four that I love.

I tell great dirty jokes.

YOUSUF KARSH

Yousuf Karsh and I became friends while I was preparing my first book of photographs, *Kenny Rogers' America*. He not only wrote the foreword for the book, but took the picture of me for the back cover as well.

Yousuf and his wife, Estrelita, came to my farm in Georgia and spent three days with me and my family. It was an experience I'll never forget. I've said it before, and I'll undoubtedly say it again: of all the great photographers in the world, Yousuf Karsh is the best at capturing not simply a person's image, but his or her *soul*. He's able to do that partly because he's so good at talking to his subjects during a session, relaxing them to the point where they'll let down their guard and reveal their true selves. It's an approach I used on certain pictures in this book, like those of Julie Harris, Linda Evans...and Yousuf Karsh. In this shot, he was talking to Rose, the makeup artist, and I was able to capture a very natural moment.

DIONNE WARWICK

It's always sad to me when anything that's truly magic ceases to exist, whatever the reasons.

When Dionne Warwick was singing the songs of Burt Bacharach and Hal David, it was just that—pure magic—and while she's done some great things since those days, I'll probably always think of Dionne in terms of "Walk On By," "Do You Know the Way to San Jose?" and all the others. I don't really know why that partnership broke up. Strangely enough, I know all three people very well, but I've never asked any of them, and none has ever offered to tell me.

Both privately and publicly, Dionne Warwick is perhaps the classiest lady in the business, so I really wanted to do something special for this shot. I must have had her in ten different poses in this chair before we found this one, as simple and obvious as it seems. The chair's design is so strong that, for better or worse, it dictated the shot entirely. It's either art nouveau or art deco. I can never tell those arts apart.

LARRY BIRD

You owe it to yourself to stand next to a professional basketball player at least once in your life. I'm six foot one, but next to Larry, who's six foot nine, I didn't feel just short—I felt like a midget.

I would have preferred to take this picture in my studio, but there wasn't time for Larry to come to me, so I went to the L.A. Sports Arena, where the Celtics were playing the Los Angeles Clippers. To me, this photo looks as if it were taken in a men's room somewhere. Actually, it was taken just outside the Celtics' locker room in a small area that was roped off for us. We were literally surrounded by the public while he was posing. It's awfully hard to be photographed with hundreds of people watching, especially when a lot of those people are taking flash pictures of their own, but Larry was terrific about it.

Larry Bird is a perfect example of someone who is at the absolute top of his profession—he was the National Basketball Association's most valuable player for three straight years—but continues to work at it. He arrived at the Sports Arena for our photo session something like three hours before the game, which left him with plenty of time to kill once we were done. I guarantee you he spent that time practicing his shooting—and as usual, he played magnificently that night.

PHIL COLLINS

Phil Collins happens to be one of my favorite singers, and not without good reason. As lead singer with Genesis, as well as in his solo career, he consistently does great songs.

Getting Phil to pose for this book was one of the strangest coincidences. My wife, Marianne, asked me if I was interested in photographing him. I said I was, but that I didn't really know him and would feel uncomfortable asking him. As fate would have it, the woman who does Marianne's nails also does Phil's mother-in-law's nails; how's that for a true Hollywood connection? Two weeks later, believe it or not, I got a call from Phil. I immediately asked who else's nails this woman did.

Bobby Daniels, the drummer in my band, does a drumstick twirling routine during our shows that the audience loves. I thought it would be great if I could photograph Phil Collins doing the same thing, so I set the lights to flash five times in rapid succession, which would capture the drumsticks in various positions while Phil remained stationary. So what happened? I told Phil what I planned to do, and he said, "Fine, but I don't know how to twirl a drumstick!" So much for that brilliant idea.

BURT REYNOLDS

       The man is a star, any way you look at it. I don't think many people are aware that Burt Reynolds was the number-one box office draw in this country for five consecutive years—a remarkable achievement, and he's the only one ever to do it. At the same time, Burt is invariably honest, which I really appreciate. Those rare times when things aren't going well, he'll tell you they aren't going well.

       I'd been thinking about his range as an actor, and I realized that while Burt may be best known for his tough-guy roles in films like *Sharkey's Machine*, he's also been in some very funny, charming comedies. I tried to have a chair available for our session that I thought would fit Burt's overall personality. I liked this ranch-style chair for him—somehow a Louis XV divan didn't seem appropriate! And since the red chair matches the red piping on his jacket, which in turn blends nicely with the red background, the shot has a nice color compatibility. This is another photograph that demanded to be in color.

AMY IRVING

I called Steven Spielberg to see if there was a chance that he and his wife, Amy Irving, along with their son, Max, might participate in the book together. Steven said that although he hates having his picture taken, he thought it was something Amy would enjoy doing. Well, that was fine with me, because I've had a crush on Amy Irving ever since she starred with Willie Nelson in the movie *Honeysuckle Rose*.

This shot is another example of the difference between my view of a person and her view of herself. I saw Amy as casual, as she did, but she saw herself in a slightly less contemporary way. We went with that, and I love the way it turned out.

There is such warmth in Amy's eyes. I get a strong sense that no matter what the problem is, she'd understand. I'm seriously considering calling Steven Spielberg to ask him if my instincts about Amy are right.

MILES DAVIS

There were three basic qualities I had in mind when selecting subjects for this project: I wanted people who were interesting-looking, talented, and well known. Miles Davis is certainly all of these.

Jazz is a unique form of music. More than any other style, it allows the opportunity for self-expression through improvisation. In fact, it *demands* it. And once a musician develops a style that's clearly his or her own, as Miles did, the legend lives forever.

As I was setting up for this photo at the Universal Amphitheatre in Los Angeles, I can't tell you how many contemporary jazz players I saw coming into the auditorium to see Miles. The man is not only a great trumpeter, but a snappy dresser as well, to say the least, and if I had this shot to do over again, I'd probably show more of his clothes. The one thing Miles jokingly worried about was that, because he was sitting down, people might think he's short. I promised I'd set the record straight: Miles Davis is six foot one.

ROBERT AND KATIE WAGNER

Having good friends is the key to success in any venture—and to fall back on another great Hollywood slogan, when you got 'em, use 'em. In this case, I did.

I called my friends Len and Wendy Goldberg, who I knew were friends of Robert's, and got them to do the advance work for me. Knowing about R.J.'s (that's more Hollywood talk) love for his daughter Katie, I thought including her would provide an incentive for him and give another dimension to the book as well.

Katie, aside from being a beautiful girl, is a true free spirit; she sports a number of tattoos, including this one on her shoulder. I remember that when I set up this photo, it was her suggestion to show it. And while I'm sure R.J. allows Katie her independence, I don't think he was wild about the idea; it always seemed to me that all he sees in this picture is Katie's tattoo. He wasn't the only one who saw it: right after this session, Rose Librizzi, my makeup artist, went out and got her own tattoo!

CESAR ROMERO

Most of the time when I'm lighting a subject, particularly a man, I'll start with a back light. I think that's where the drama of a photo is created.

With Cesar Romero, I used the system I call layered lighting, which uses a minimum of three and preferably four zones, or grades of light, on the face. It helped to have a subject with as handsome and striking a face as Cesar's. His eyes are especially good for the layered technique because they catch the light so well.

People who only know Cesar from *Falcon Crest* might be surprised to know how long and varied a career he's had. As we talked, he told me about the movies he made with some of the great screen sirens of all time, like Carole Lombard, Greer Garson, Marlene Dietrich, Barbara Stanwyck, Betty Grable, and Alice Fay. Obviously, he still looks terrific. That old saying "I hope I look that good when I'm his age" simply doesn't apply to him. The truth is, I wish I looked that good *now*.

LAFFIT PINCAY, JR., AND WILLIE SHOEMAKER

Competition is a strange animal. I've seen people who normally have a great deal in common refuse to speak to each other for fear of giving away the competitive edge. How refreshing it is to see that two guys who fight each other with a vengeance on the track can be such good friends when the race is over.

This photo had to be taken twice. In order to get the jockeys in their silks and their natural environment, I went to Santa Anita racetrack. The first time, I took a 4 x 5 camera because of its portability, hoping it would be sufficient, but the quality suffered greatly in comparison to the 8 x 10. All's well that ends well, though. In the first picture, the wall behind them was blank. When I went back with the 8 x 10, I found the racing mural in the business office, and I think it makes a major difference to the shot. Most people, in fact, think there's an actual race in progress.

Incidentally, I bet six races that day—and I lost six races that day. This was a very expensive photo.

CLINT EASTWOOD

It's a true dichotomy: Dirty Harry and His Honor, Mayor Clint Eastwood. The two are so different that I had no real idea how to approach this photograph—and since the session took place on very short notice, I didn't have much time to think it over. As luck would have it, I walked into my living room and saw these two huge, cast-iron winged lions. It suddenly hit me that they had just the right feeling of strength I wanted for him.

I had been trying to get together with Clint for a good seven months, and during that entire time his office would call me at least twice a week in an attempt to coordinate our schedules. They couldn't have been more helpful. As it turned out, Clint was in Los Angeles one day to help out with Nancy Reagan's antidrug campaign. He called me up and said, "Well, I'm in town, I've got a suit on, and there are no stains on my tie yet, so how's today?"

The Dirty Harry movies are some of my favorites. One-on-one, Clint is so warm and personable that he makes you feel you know him much better than you really do. At one point I asked him why he had run for mayor of Carmel, California, and he said, "Sometimes if you want to see a change for the better, you have to take things into your own hands." To me, that's classic Clint Eastwood. And coincidentally, classic Dirty Harry.

WHOOPI GOLDBERG

I love the shot of Whoopi Goldberg by Annie Leibovitz, with Whoopi stretched out in a bathtub filled with milk, only her head, arms, and legs showing. But I'm simply not capable of a shot like that, and I don't think it would suit my style at all. What I wanted was something that might be less daring, but would also reveal Whoopi's whimsy, and especially her warmth of character.

Every time I finish a portrait, I send a print over to the person and ask him or her to sign it so I can frame it and hang it in my studio in Los Angeles. Whoopi's message, I think, says a lot about both her and the picture: "This seems to be the real me," she wrote, "trying to figure out what's coming up next to me."

JON VOIGHT

I got a surprise phone call from Jon Voight one day. Having recently watched most of my own films on television, somehow I knew he wasn't calling me to be in a movie with him. What he wanted involved something that's very important to him: he wanted me to participate in a concert in Washington, D.C., to help Vietnam War veterans.

Jon's tough character in *Runaway Train,* his latest film at the time he called me, hardly prepared me for the very caring person I eventually met. The more we talked about various projects close to us, the more I learned about him and enjoyed him. I was in the process of doing a movie about the problems of the American Indian, and I was impressed once again with his knowledge and concern about this sensitive social issue. In the end, we spent very little time on photography and a lot of time talking about these more important matters.

WOODY HERMAN

       I vividly remember going to hear Woody Herman's big band years ago and sitting eight feet away from his legendary saxophone section, who were known as the Four Brothers. It was an awesome sound. By then, Woody had already been a major jazz figure for a long time (his first hit, "Woodchopper's Ball," was recorded in 1939), and it was in his band that brilliant musicians like Stan Getz, Milt Jackson, Terry Gibbs, and Zoot Sims got early national exposure. So it was with great respect that I invited Woody to be in this book, and I was very proud when he accepted.

       It was also a somewhat sad occasion, because several conversations I had with Woody helped confirm my fear that the big band era is very likely coming to a close. It is no longer practical to take fifteen or twenty musicians around the world on a long tour; you can't generate the kind of income needed to keep that many people on the road. My own experience has shown me that it can cost more than $100,000 per person, all things considered, to tour for a year. It's also hard to find young guys who are willing to pay years of dues playing in relative obscurity in a big band. Woody Herman is one of the very few leaders who's been able to keep a band working. I'm grateful to him.

EVA GABOR

This picture was the first "set piece" I arranged for the book, and it probably has a more formal setup than any other photograph. I'd just been looking at some old George Hurrell portraits when Eva and I got together, and I suppose I was trying to capture the Hurrell style and create a living room atmosphere. As far as I'm concerned, the shot borders on being too busy, but Eva's one of the few who can successfully pull it off.

To most Americans, Eva may still be best known for her role on *Green Acres*, with Eddie Albert. Looking at her here, in all her elegance, you must admit it's hard to imagine this woman wallowing around on television with a pig named Arnold. Somehow, I think Eva would prefer to be remembered in a glamorous pose—and I assure you, *this* is the real Eva Gabor.

GREGORY PECK

I think I did everything I could to try to ruin this picture. I had this image in my mind of Gregory Peck in front of a case of antique books, reading, with his glasses on. Because of that, I ended up in a small, confined area, with no way to backlight or create any layered-lighting effect for the shot. And as if that wasn't bad enough, Greg's dog, who has only three legs because of an accident when he was a puppy, was determined to be in the picture. And for the better part of thirty minutes I was determined he wouldn't be.

It wasn't until I looked through the lens to see how I could exclude the dog that I realized how much he really added. So now, if anyone comments on the shot, I say, "And wasn't that a great idea I had to put the dog in there?"

RACHEL McLISH

It's funny, but a lot of men I know called to offer their assistance when they found out I was going to photograph bodybuilder Rachel McLish. I had seen Rachel on several television shows, and I am always impressed by someone who has the discipline to work out—I mean, I can work out, but to *continue* working out is something else entirely.

I wanted to capture Rachel's body as if it were a statue, and this base added the right classical touch. It's the first body shot I've ever done, and Rachel was very helpful; I used fourteen lights, and while I worked at setting them just right, she would hold this position for an extraordinary length of time.

Before every shot, Rachel would do thirty-five or forty regular push-ups and a set of one-handed push-ups. She was concerned about what's called an "uneven pump." As you can see, all her weight is on her right hand and left foot, so the blood is draining out of her left arm. Rachel was worried that her right arm would show this great muscularity while the left wouldn't. I was exhausted just watching her.

I have a friend who photographs nude layouts for *Playboy,* and I asked his wife once if she didn't occasionally get jealous. She said that he'd assured her that you don't really see the bodies; you see the overall composition. I can honestly tell you that I was concentrating so hard at the time that I did not fully appreciate Rachel's body until I printed this picture. I *think* Marianne will believe that.

LILY TOMLIN

Sometimes in photography, there's a fine line between being prepared and being *too* prepared, too locked in to a concept for a picture. I think that's especially true with entertainers, because one never knows how much of what they present reflects what they really are.

I had considered trying a multiple exposure of three of Lily's characters on one page (and using three different-sized and -shaped picture frames to display them), or at least a multiple flash image photo. But both concepts were very time-consuming and, to say the least, rather risky. When she came to the studio, I didn't have the nerve to suggest a complicated session; although Lily gave me no reason to believe she was in a hurry, she had just come from doing the Joan Rivers show, and it was late at night. The 8 x 10 camera was a factor, too, as it simply doesn't allow much room for spontaneous experimentation.

There was an interesting moment when we got started: Lily wasn't sure what I wanted, and I wasn't sure how to ask her. My concern was that she would feel I wanted a typical shot, which I guess I did; and *her* concern was that she felt a little silly suggesting "Ernestine" and "Edith Anne." But once we agreed on who and how we were shooting, she really came to life and was amazingly inventive with the telephone cord and picture frame, all aspects of her characters. There are some people you need to create for, and others you need to allow to create for themselves. Lily Tomlin needs no help.

LINDA EVANS

I give up. How can a woman who eats pizza every night have a body like this? When Linda Evans and I worked together in the second television movie based on "The Gambler," I became her pizza connection. I'd order a pizza for myself and an extra one for Linda—and I'm talking the works, including anchovies. You can see what it did to me, but Linda still looks great. I have a tremendous amount of resentment toward her for that.

I was very comfortable calling Linda to be in this book, in part because of our friendship and in part because I knew that it's virtually impossible to get a bad shot of her. I soon found out why that's true. Apart from the obvious—her beauty—Linda is also one of the most cooperative and gracious subjects for any photographer. She was in the studio for six and a half hours (needless to say, this was before I started promising people that a session would take no more than thirty minutes!) and we did three or four different setups. So Linda's innate understanding of herself, combined with the fact that she gives a photographer enough time to do his best work, ensures a good shot. And working with Linda helped give me the confidence I needed for the rest of the book.

PAUL SIMON

It was the classic conflict: art vs. commerce, creativity vs. money. Paul Simon was in the middle of his *Graceland* tour and was performing in Los Angeles. I had gotten permission to photograph him backstage at the Universal Amphitheatre and proceeded to set up my equipment in front of this incredible bank of multicolored lights. Just as we were preparing to shoot, I was politely informed by a union representative that I couldn't shoot backstage unless I paid a fee. No problem, I figured, until I was told that the fee was $1700. Seventeen hundred dollars! I said thanks but no thanks, and with the help of Paul's road crew I moved the setup about fifty feet away to an area that was no longer considered "backstage."

Of course, Paul couldn't resist saying, "As much money as you make, you wouldn't pay seventeen hundred dollars to take my picture?" In the end, we got a picture that was close to what I'd originally envisioned anyway. And if you ever get a chance to see Paul Simon under any conditions, by all means do it.

THE POINTER SISTERS

June, Ruth, and Anita Pointer: without question, they are the three most colorful women I've ever met, both personally and physically. The chairs they're sitting on in this photo were actually painted after they arrived, while they were busy doing their makeup. But I soon learned that wet paint will never stop the Pointer Sisters.

I wanted personality from the Pointers, and believe me, that's what I got. In fact, I got three very distinct personalities, and the hardest part was controlling them to the point where I could get a picture that made sense. Once you organize the chaos, you can really feel their energy. I had to be a physical editor here, so to speak, isolating a movement from each woman and having her hold it until I got the other two in complementary poses.

The electricity just flowed from these three, and I was exhausted when the session was over. A warning: any photographer who dares get in the same room with the Pointer Sisters is taking his life into his own hands!

BARBARA MANDRELL

Ironically, some of the hardest people actually to get into the studio for this book were the friends I've known the longest. It's not that they didn't want to do it. I think friends simply feel more comfortable saying, "Look, it's just not convenient for me today," whereas someone you don't have a long-term relationship with might feel an obligation to do it even when it's inconvenient. Consequently, making an arrangement with a friend can end up taking a little longer.

It's a good thing there are awards shows and other special events because otherwise I'm not sure there would have been a convenient time to do Barbara, since she lives in Nashville and I live in L.A. We managed to hook up when she was in town the night before the People's Choice Awards ceremony.

Barbara's face is so photogenic that I don't think it's possible to get a bad picture of her. She also loves to experiment with her appearance. I found this "look" in a magazine, so we robbed Marianne's closet at midnight to get the right clothes.

LITTLE RICHARD

Very few people can honestly say they've been responsible for affecting the world in any lasting fashion. Richard Penniman, better known as Little Richard, can say that without false modesty. Along with a small handful of others, he quite literally changed the course of modern music.

Richard is excitement personified, so I certainly wasn't going to let him just stand there. In order to capture some movement, I ended up using a combination of strobe lights on his face and body, and a tungsten light on his hand. I also used an inordinately long exposure: one second, as I remember.

What a thrill this was! I probably took longer than necessary on this shot, just so I could hear him play. After all, how many times do you get a private performance of "Tutti Frutti" and "Good Golly, Miss Molly"?

JOAN RIVERS

When Joan Rivers agreed to be in the book, I told her that she could bring either her dog or her husband, Edgar. I think it says something about Joan that for her, the choice was simple: she brought the dog.

Joan had just started doing her nightly television show when we got together. I think she was still in her hostess frame of mind when she arrived at the studio, because the whole time we were there, she was interviewing me about the people I'd already photographed: who was the most interesting, the least interesting, the most fun, and, of course, the most trouble.

One quality of Joan's I really admire is her candor. By her own admission, she's had quite a bit of cosmetic surgery, and her attitude is "OK, I did it, and I don't care who knows it." If people want to dig up some dirt about you, they'll do it. So instead of being shocked and angry when you see your name in a lurid tabloid headline, why not just be honest and up-front? If you tell the truth, it's harder for people to invent lies. I think Joan is very secure and strong—and she's got a great-looking dog. Sorry, Edgar.

CARY GRANT AND
BARBARA GRANT

When I started work on this book, there was a handful of people who I knew from the beginning I would have to have. Cary Grant was one of them.

I'd known Cary and Barbara for five years, and I genuinely felt that he did not like to be photographed in his last few years—amazing when you consider that even in his eighties, he was one of the most handsome men alive. One of the things that made it worthwhile for him to be in the book, I think, was the opportunity to appear with Barbara, who was so important to him. They were obviously very close. When Barbara had to move to another part of my studio to adjust her makeup, Cary laughed, put his chin in his hands, and said, "Well, I'm left again."

Two weeks after we got together, sad to say, Cary died. To the very end, he was the epitome of a movie star: suave, debonair, a handsome lady-killer.

ELIZABETH TAYLOR

When you're photographing one of the world's most beautiful women, you don't just bring her in, throw up a few lights, load your film, and shoot away. Elizabeth Taylor has been shot by the best photographers in the world. You see very few bad photos of her—and you sure don't want yours to be one of them.

I had seen this fine piece of etched glass before and felt it added to the elegance of the composition I had in mind. Even though Elizabeth was two hours late to the session (with good cause), the truth is that I loved having the extra time to fine-tune the lighting, especially the effect of the color gels on the glass; and since I was shooting with six lights, it required extra precautions.

Elizabeth was totally gracious. People who have had their picture taken so many times occasionally try to direct a photo session. I may be the worst culprit of all. But Elizabeth offered input, not direction; she was helpful instead of intimidating. I'm grateful for that. I also admire her tremendously as someone who has her life completely under control, who has revealed a resilience and inner strength that few of us possess. To me, she still looks as stunning as she did when she was the most beautiful teenager ever.

HUGH HEFNER

I've always thought Hugh Hefner has movie star–quality looks, and that made him a natural for this book. But our life-styles are, well, different. Put it this way: this picture was taken at 5:30 in the afternoon, and I'm still not sure whether Hef was getting up or going to bed.

The other color pictures in the book tend to have very rich, vivid schemes. This one is more muted, due to the gray walls, the brown door, and Hef's lavender shirt and robe; yet despite the subtlety, I think it's a striking shot. It's also one of the very few photographs in the book that was taken outdoors.

JANE SEYMOUR

Jane Seymour is English, as you know, and I'd originally planned on shooting her in front of an English wall-hanging depicting a classic hunting scene. Obviously, I wasn't the only one with that idea: Jane told me that in the last six sessions she'd done, the photographers had used a tapestry! So she suggested doing her portrait in another, less formal way, and we agreed that showing her with her ballet shoes hanging over her shoulder would be a nice touch. An appropriate one, too: Jane is a trained dancer and would probably have pursued ballet as a career if not for a serious knee injury she suffered as a teenager.

I love Jane's hair, so shooting her in profile made sense. What's more, her face is not only very pretty, but beautifully shaped as well, and I thought we might show it to better effect from the side. That also meant using a couple of interesting but more complicated lighting techniques: we put a tungsten on her hair and a small spotlight on the shoes.

Ah, the things we photographers go through for beautiful women.

FRANK SINATRA

There's no doubt about it: "Ol' Blue Eyes" still sings better than anyone in the business.

I went to the Golden Nugget Hotel in Las Vegas to take this shot. I watched both shows that night, and I'll tell you, no one comes close to Frank Sinatra. As I listened to him, I wondered if people loved the old songs, or if it was simply that they loved Frank. I'm convinced that people love *anything* Frank Sinatra does.

Frank was, and always has been, very gracious to me. He suggested that we wait until after his second show to do the photo, because his daughter Nancy and his granddaughters were to have dinner with him. I set up all my gear in the hotel's executive offices and waited until 1:00 A.M. When Frank arrived, we did two setups, one with him holding a microphone and this one with a slot machine. He called the "one-armed bandit" a perfect prop for him, but somehow I can't imagine Frank Sinatra standing in the casino playing a quarter slot machine.

Not long after I took this photo I got a call from Nancy, who wondered if I'd be interested in recording a country duet with Frank for an album project he's putting together. I've recorded a lot of duets in my time, but this one would be hard to top. I'll do it no matter how busy I am. After all, how do you say no to Frank Sinatra—and why would you?

PRISCILLA PRESLEY

I pictured Priscilla Presley with her hair blowing back, wearing a big hoop earring, a gold choker, and a gold spaghetti-strap blouse I had found. It would have made a striking high-fashion shot.

But I also asked the people in this book to bring things with them for their portraits that would reflect the way they see themselves. In Priscilla's case, she brought the rose, the hat, the dress—everything but the mirror, which I found in the storage room in the building that houses my studio.

Photographically speaking, I think this view of Priscilla turned out to be the better one. But to me, the most interesting point is that Priscilla sees herself this way. That shows you how far apart one man's perception and one woman's reality can be.

WALTER MATTHAU

In Hollywood, you never know who you'll meet at the next party. Marianne and I were invited to a Christmas gathering at Barbara and Marvin Davis' (Marvin runs 20th Century Fox). Walter Matthau was there with his wife, Carol, and that led to Walter's being in the book. The truth is I couldn't take my eyes off this man all night. I've loved every movie he's ever made, but to me Walter will always be Kotch, a character from the movie of the same name. And, somehow, the parts he plays tend to remind me of my father.

Almost everyone whose picture I've taken for the book has been concerned about what to wear. I guess most of them, like me, usually have pictures taken for a purpose, like movie publicity or an album cover. And in the case of actors, they're often posing as a specific character, with someone else dictating their wardrobe. That makes it hard for them to know how they want to be presented in a personal portrait. The day Walter came to my studio, it had been raining. He brought several hanging bags full of clothing, but we used none of it. What you see here is exactly what he wore when he came through the door out of the rain. That's the Walter Matthau I wanted to show.

LUCILLE BALL

There are very few entertainers for whom a single name means instant recognition. Sinatra is one…and Lucille Ball is another. Simply say the name Lucy, and millions of people will know exactly who you're talking about. Now *that's* stature.

Lucy and I have sat next to each other at a charity function in Denver called the Carousel Ball for the last five years, so I've had a chance to enjoy her humor firsthand. For this shot I went to the set of her new television show, which she had just started working on. People kept apologizing to me because they were running late; I had to wait an hour or so, but I really enjoyed just sitting back and watching her be Lucy. She's a very vibrant, spontaneous person who, like all of us who perform, lives for that applause and that time spent onstage.

Because she was in the middle of taping an episode, I set up my equipment right next to the set. It got a little crazy, because the whole time we were shooting, Lucy had to keep running back to the set for additional takes, which meant that we were only able to fit in a shot or two between interruptions. But Lucy was marvelous about it, totally accommodating and professional. It was a treat for me simply to be around someone whose appeal has endured for better than three decades. I was disappointed when her show didn't take off, but Lucille Ball has still got it.

JOHN FORSYTHE

I had a very specific mental image of John Forsythe before I took his picture. Like most people, I saw him as Blake Carrington on *Dynasty:* suave, sophisticated, someone who would be as comfortable in a tuxedo as you or I might be in an old sweatshirt.

Actually, John and I did talk about doing the picture with him wearing a white dinner jacket. He told me he had one and would bring it along, but apparently he couldn't find it. And in any case, I think he saw himself more as a ranch hand.

To me, John's light-colored jacket is a little too dominant here. The color is really powder blue, but in black and white, it's a little less effective than it would be in color. And yet, every time I'm about to say of a certain picture, "Boy, I'd love to reshoot this one," someone comes along and says, "You know, that's one of my favorite photographs." That was precisely the case with this picture.

Most of all, I'm grateful I had the chance to work with John. When I began this book, I had a few criteria for choosing people to photograph: an interesting face, a certain celebrity stature. But in some cases, I simply chose people I wanted to meet. John Forsythe was one of them.

LIONEL HAMPTON

If there's a single question I'm asked most often, it's probably "Why do you work so much?" My answer is simple, and I assume it would be the same for Lionel Hampton, who at the age of seventy-eight still performs 150 concerts a year. You don't stop doing something just because you're successful at it. You don't stop working just because you can afford to; you work because it keeps you young—it's a reason to get up in the morning. I assure you, Lionel will play as long as someone will listen. That's what makes him Lionel Hampton, the best (and unquestionably the best-known) vibraphone player ever.

He is another person I'd always wanted to meet, but probably never would have without this book as an excuse. During the session we reminisced about the "good old days" of jazz and found we had a mutual friend in Arnett Cobb, who I worked with in Houston, where I played stand-up bass in jazz groups for ten years. Arnett was the tenor sax player on Lionel's all-time classic recording of "Flying Home."

Lionel stood and played for the better part of an hour while we set up our lights for the shot. If you still wonder why he works so much, just take a look at his face while he's playing.

PRESIDENT JIMMY CARTER

Being a former President would appear to be as hectic as being President. When I got together with President Carter at the Carter Presidential Center in Atlanta, a photographer was taking pictures of his wife, Rosalynn, in another room; the crew from *20/20* was following Mr. Carter around for a segment they were preparing; and there was an in-house photographer taking pictures of *us* taking pictures. I could barely keep it all straight.

My camera was set up in President Carter's personal office. We had to move every piece of furniture in the room to organize the shot; he was great about the whole thing. In fact, I tried to talk him into leaving it that way, with chairs piled up on top of one another—a piece of modern art.

The rocking chair was a gift from Sam Maloof, a California artist and woodworker. Behind the President is an oil painting of Rosalynn and Amy Carter by Thornton Utz. As for the lilies, they were included not so much for their beauty (even though it was a week before Easter), but to hide one of my pet peeves: an electrical outlet. In retrospect, I think they add a nice warmth.

The photo session itself was easy. Rearranging Mr. Carter's office, however, may have done irreparable damage to my body.

JANET JACKSON

For the longest time she was known merely as Michael Jackson's little sister, but certainly not anymore. By virtue of the *Control* album, Janet Jackson has become a dominant force in pop music. And you only have to see a few seconds of her in performance to realize that Janet, like the rest of the Jackson family, has all the right moves.

I wanted to use a very high tech approach for this shot. But as much as I'd like to take credit for the technique we used, I have to admit that it was my assistant Bernie Boudreau's brainchild.

The circle behind Janet is nothing more than a fluorescent tube covered with blue and red gel filters, with a quarter-inch space between the gels to create the white lines. Once we established our strobe exposures, we shot Polaroids at various shutter speeds to determine how best to expose the fluorescent tube. The shot itself required two separate exposures, first for the strobes (without modeling lights) and second with Bernie moving in behind Janet, who held her pose while we opened the shutter to expose the tube. It was a painstaking job, but I think the result is unique.

Janet is a dynamic performer, but surprisingly, she's very soft-spoken and shy offstage. I think Janet is a prime example of an entertainer who is simply transformed when the lights go up. And when they go up on Janet Jackson, look out!

BARRY MANILOW

One of the nice things about the 8 x 10 format is the actual physical distance it places between the camera and the subject. With a 35mm camera the photographer is right in your face, constantly snapping away. But the 8 x 10 is fairly far away from the subject, which provides a certain breath of air, a comfort zone. There's also much more time between shots, which allows a person to relax, collect himself, and consider a different look.

The advantages of the 8 x 10 were especially apparent when I shot Barry Manilow. We did six shots, and of the six, this is the only one where Barry's tie wasn't hanging straight down the middle. I think people see him as very organized, with everything right where it's supposed to be. Yet when I see him, I see a little disorganization—that's one of the things I like about him. This shot shows that inconsistency, and I probably wouldn't have gotten it with a small-format camera.

Barry has told me that this is his favorite picture of himself. When I sent him a copy, I wrote on it, "Dear Barry: If I'm not mistaken, you're supposed to face the other way when you play piano."

SAMMY DAVIS, JR.

I remember the first time I saw Sammy Davis, Jr., on television. He sang, played drums, danced, and basically did everything anybody—or any three people—could want to do, only better. As a would-be entertainer myself, I thought he was the most talented person I'd ever seen, and he did it all with such ease.

When I called Sammy about being in the book, I started in on my pitch about who else would be taking part, how quickly we could get it done, and so forth. Sammy stopped me and said, "If you're doing it, that's all I need to know. Just tell me when and where, and I'll be there." That meant a lot to me.

Sammy told a lot of stories during our session, and one of them involved the walking stick he's holding here. Seems he was on a trip to Africa and happened to meet Jomo Kenyatta, the great leader who negotiated Kenya's independence in 1963. Sammy went up to him and began to introduce himself, but before he could get his name out, Kenyatta interrupted him and said, "Sammy Davis, Jr.!" Now that's what I call fame. Kenyatta gave him the walking stick, and Sammy's obviously very proud of it.

DON HENLEY

One of the great joys of the music business is that occasionally you meet someone before he finds himself, or at least before the rest of the world discovers his talent.

I met Don Henley in 1969, while I was with the First Edition. He lived in a little town called Linden, Texas, and was working with a group called Felicity. From the moment I heard him sing and play drums, I genuinely felt he was special. As a member of the Eagles, he went on to write (with Glenn Frey) what may be my favorite song ever: "Desperado."

I shot Don twice, using the same setup each time. The first time, the mirror was exactly symmetrical behind him, with one reflection on each side. But I prefer not to have perfect symmetry in my photographs, so the second time I arranged the mirror so there would be two reflections on the left. A minor adjustment, but I like it better this way.

VINCENTE MINNELLI

There are times as a photographer when you see a once-in-a-lifetime picture that somehow cannot or will not be shot. I met Vincente Minnelli about five years ago, and my family and I had been invited to join him for Christmas dinner for several years. It was Christmas of '85 when I walked into the living room of Vincente and his wife Lee's home and encountered just such a once-in-a-lifetime circumstance.

There was Liza Minnelli, the superstar, sitting on the floor at the feet of her aging father, curled up near his legs and gazing up at him as she must have done as a child. I wanted more than anything to photograph that scene and tried to arrange to do so for the better part of a year. But due to a combination of Liza's and my schedules and Vincente's declining health, I eventually realized it wasn't going to happen.

Despite feeling very poorly, Vincente agreed to come to the studio. When I took this shot, he had just been awarded the French Legion of Honor (the highest honor given by the French government) for *An American in Paris,* which is just one of the brilliant films he directed. The award is the small pin you can see in his lapel, and he was very proud of it. But he was even prouder of Liza. When I mentioned that I had shot her for this book as well and planned to show his portrait to her, Vincente's face lit up with pleasure. Happily, I was able to capture that expression on film. A special thanks to his wife, Lee, for helping to make this happen.

JANE FONDA

Sometimes it pays to be flexible. Jane was on her way to a formal event when she stopped by my studio. She had brought her evening clothes, but we both opted for the jeans and jacket she was wearing at the time. Since I had already planned and lit two totally different concepts that would work with an evening gown, but certainly not with jeans, that decision meant I had to reorient my thinking totally (and quickly), but the end result was well worth it.

I had met Jane and her husband, Tom Hayden, on several occasions, but while we had spoken, I couldn't honestly say we were friends. If you're lucky, though, you can get one-on-one with someone for even a short time and end up feeling as if you've gotten a tremendous amount of insight into that person. This was one of those times. And as I look at the picture, I can see so much of Henry Fonda in his daughter's eyes. Just one thing kept bothering me while we were together, though: I couldn't help thinking, "Now here's a woman with probably the best body in Hollywood, and she's made millions with it. So what am I doing hiding it behind jeans and a leather jacket? Something's wrong here."

TONY CURTIS

I have long been a fan of Tony Curtis' movies, especially the classic *Some Like It Hot*. But what I didn't know is that Tony is also a skilled and accomplished painter. In fact, he was in the midst of preparations for a fifty-piece show of his work in Hawaii. I was very impressed by that. Photography is one thing, but fifty is a lot of paintings.

When he came to the studio, Tony was wearing a black jacket, a black scarf around his neck, and a white polo shirt. We kept stripping him down until he was wearing just this white ribbed t-shirt. He's very proud of the condition of his body, and well he should be: he's in great shape.

I think this is the first time Tony has been photographed with his paintings. He brought six or eight with him, which was more than we could use for the design I had in mind. He had trouble deciding which ones not to use, since he has such personal feelings about each painting. I finally made the choice for him. It was equally hard for me, and I didn't even have to worry about personal attachments.

LIZA MINNELLI

Before taking this picture, I went to see Liza perform at the Universal Amphitheatre in Los Angeles. When I know I'm going to photograph people, it helps to see them in their own environment, at home or at work, to get some sense of what they're all about and how much or how little they'll be willing to do in front of a camera. At one point in the show, Liza struck this exact pose—and to me, at least, it represented what she is all about: talent, grace, elegance.

The backdrop is nothing more than two 4x8 sheets of gator board. I had a local artist friend come in and draw the skyline, an abstract representation of New York. By painting some of the buildings with different thicknesses of paint and backlighting the whole scene, we were able to create the illusion of depth. By the way, the song "New York, New York" is also classic Liza.

GOVERNOR JOHN Y. BROWN
AND PHYLLIS GEORGE BROWN

I will never ever again shoot a photograph without proper equipment.

John Y. and Phyllis George Brown have been friends of mine for at least seven years, and they were spending Easter weekend with my family at our farm in Georgia. John was running for governor of Kentucky again this year, and he asked if I'd take his official campaign portrait. The deal was that I'd do the portrait and then take a picture of John and Phyllis together. I jokingly told John that if he was reelected, I'd include them in the book—but if he lost, they were out.

After piecing together several different power packs and strobe heads with burned-out modeling lights, we started shooting at about three o'clock in the afternoon. Three hours later, I suggested we take a break for dinner. I was very discouraged, because everything I'd planned seemed so contrived, so stock. But John Y. and Phyllis were absolute champs; no other couple could have had a better attitude. And since they're both so photogenic, the blame fell squarely on my shoulders. Just as I was telling Marianne how depressed I was, I saw this mirror and chair in her bathroom. What had been missing, I realized, was a sense of architecture, and these items solved the problem.

JOHN TRAVOLTA

I've always felt that people who have spent a lot of time in front of a camera have an inherent sense of when they look good. John Travolta does. He had a definite idea of how he wanted to project himself, and he had an instinctive feel for when the look was right to take the picture.

When he's not working, John is in one of his airplanes. Flying for him is like photography for me—not merely a diversion, but a passion—and he's an accomplished pilot. He brought three model planes to our photography session as a personal touch, but they just didn't work. As an alternative, I arranged a lighting scheme that was originally set to have John looking straight into the camera. For some reason, before he came I'd decided to use a "plume" soft box for the right side of his face. When we shot, John instinctively looked off-camera, and the result was a whole different feel—one very much like a George Hurrell photo, I think. Another interesting aspect: I kept trying to put a silver concho belt on him, but John didn't like the idea. Now that I see the photo, I realize he was right.

JONATHAN WINTERS

I made one fatal mistake when I called Jonathan Winters to be in the book: I asked him how he was. He immediately went off into a fifteen-minute monologue about how the Indians had him surrounded, and if we didn't come and rescue him right away they'd have his scalp. But that's Jonathan. He is one of the most spontaneously creative people I've ever met, and it takes nothing to set him off. In fact, after faithfully promising him that he'd be out of the studio in thirty minutes, I had to *push* him out two hours later.

His son is a professional baseball player, and Jonathan showed up wearing this Cincinnati Reds uniform. He then *became* Babe Ruth; the resemblance was truly uncanny. He even did one pose that echoed the famous "called shot," when Ruth pointed to the bleachers where he planned to hit a home run, and then did it. Jonathan went through about twelve other characters as well, all of which had everyone in the studio in stitches. It was a great two hours.

DOLLY PARTON

What can you say about Dolly? She may have the best-known body in the world, but I think there's a tendency to underrate her singing and songwriting. Behind that remarkable, effervescent personality is a great artist, which is too often overlooked.

It was very important to me not to do the same type of shot I've seen so much in Dolly's publicity photos, where her cleavage is the center of attention. What I hoped to capture was a special quality — a quality not only of talent and style but of complete self-assurance — that I've come to see in Dolly as we've worked together in the last couple of years. I think I succeeded.

Early in 1986, I toured Australia with Dolly during the America's Cup competition. The reviewers killed me and loved her. After that, I think I can understand what Iain Murray, the Australian skipper, meant when he said, "I did the best I could. I was just chasing a better boat."

MUHAMMAD ALI

Muhammad Ali was the greatest, is the greatest, and will always be the greatest. The man is the P.T. Barnum of boxing, and I confess that I'm one of the millions of people he manipulated when he was in his prime. I bet against him every fight because I didn't believe he could do all the things he bragged about. But he could—and as the saying goes, it's not bragging if you can do it.

Believe it or not, I used to be a boxer: I fought in the light-heavyweight class in high school. I thought I was pretty good, too. But when a kid who weighed about 130 pounds beat me to a bloody pulp one day, I started wondering what someone my own size could do to me, and that was the end of my boxing career. I guess *I* was bragging.

Muhammad is a complex, sensitive man. Kelly Junkermann, one of my assistants, wanted him to sign a boxing glove. Muhammad took the glove and wrote not only "To Kelly—with love, Muhammad Ali," but also this: "Love is the net that catches hearts like fish." It was very, very touching.

Then there's his other, more familiar side. In the midst of our photo session, Muhammad called me over and whispered, "Kenny, I am one bad dude." I couldn't agree more.

GEORGE HURRELL

George Hurrell has probably shot more great Hollywood stars than any photographer alive. His style virtually defined portraiture in the thirties and forties: his use of multiple lights for a hotter, harder look remained the standard for photographers until people like Richard Avedon, who used just one light for portrait shooting, came along in the sixties. When I first started seriously considering doing this book, I bought every volume of portraits I could lay my hands on—and it's no coincidence that the photos I consistently came back to were George Hurrell's.

George works only with tungsten lights, while I work mostly with strobes. Our equipment is certainly different; when George shot me, he used a wooden 8 x 10 camera with a meter and lights that are decades old, while my gear is modern and computer controlled. Yet our objectives are similar. When you're dealing with celebrities or other strong personalities, it's essential to get a picture that flatters them or at the very least represents them in a way that makes them happy and comfortable. George is a master at doing that. What's more, his continuing enthusiasm for the work is an inspiration to me, because I plan on having photography as a creative outlet long after my musical career is over.

It gives me great satisfaction to know that I've learned—and stolen—from the very best.

GEORGE BURNS

George Burns is amazing. I swear, the man has probably had more dates with beautiful women in the last six months than I had in my entire life before I got married. He is the most phenomenal human being I've ever met—of *any* age. My guess is that George will still be here when I'm gone, still dating girls younger than me.

The moment I called George to be in the book, he said, "Absolutely. When and where?" I knew what I wanted to capture: this smiling man with the glasses and the cigar, which he smokes incessantly. And I got it almost immediately. He couldn't have been in the studio more than ten minutes. I think he knows that all he has to do is be George Burns.

MARIANNE ROGERS

You've heard the old saying that a cobbler's children have no shoes. Well, in this case the photographer's wife has no pictures. Marianne, the most beautiful woman in the world (in my opinion) and certainly one of the most photogenic, will not let me take her photograph. She'll happily sit in Harry Langdon's studio and let him play with his lights for eight hours; I'm lucky to get twelve minutes. Put it this way: Marianne's the type who double-parks when she comes to a photo session with me.

It means a great deal to me to include Marianne in this book, because aside from being my wife she's also my friend. And she has been very supportive of this project, encouraging me when I was down, helping arrange for certain people to take part, always making constructive suggestions when I'd lost my own objectivity. *Your Friends and Mine* is as much Marianne's book as mine, for the simple truth is that I could not have done it without her.

Designed by John Coulter
Photographic prints by Bernard Boudreau, Brad Cole, and Kenny Rogers
Black-and-white photographs reproduced in the Laser Fultones® process
Color photographs laser-scanned and reproduced in 200-line screen
Printed by Gardner Lithograph on 100 lb. Centura Gloss Book
Text set in American Gothic Medium by Aldus Type Sudio, Ltd.
Bound by Horowitz/Rae Book Manufacturers, Inc.